Changing Seasons

Changing Seasons

John E. Smelcer

SOUTH HEAD PRESS

Berrima, Australia

Grateful acknowledgement is made to the following periodicals and anthologies in which many of these poems first appeared:

The American Voice, The Amicus Journal, Artful Dodge, The Atlantic Monthly, The Beloit Poetry Journal, The Christian Science Monitor, The Detroit Writer's Project, Dog River Review, Explorations, Faultline, Heartland, The Journal of Alaska Native Arts, The Kenyon Review, The Literary Review, Lost Creek Letters, Permafrost, Poet, Poets On:, Poetpourri, Poetry Australia, Raven Chronicles, Rosebud, Transnational Perspectives, The Tucumcari Literary Review & ZYZZYVA.

"Changing Seasons," "Father," "Potlatch," "Resurrected," "Ritual" and "Talt'aezi Bene' Xeltse'e" appeared in *Everything Matters: Auto-biographical Essays By Native American Writers* (Random House).

"Weir Fisher," "Dadzaasi Luk'ae," "Potlatch" and "Evening at Fielding Lake" appeared in *Koht'aene Kenaege'* (R. L. Barth Press).

"Dadzaasi Luk'ae," "Homeland," "Lost Notion," "Resurrected" and "The Road to Chitina" appeared in *IKTOMI* (translated into Russian).

"Changing Seasons," "Durable Breath," "Kesugi Ridge," "Tern Creek" and "Weir Fisher" appeared in *Durable Breath: Contemporary Native American Poetry* (Salmon Run Press & American Indian Press).

"Ceremony" appeared in *North Of Eden* (Loose Affiliation Press).

The author wishes to thank the following individuals for their support: Molly Peacock, Ursula K. LeGuin, Joy Harjo, Joe Bruchac, X. J. Kennedy, Peter Davison, Ruth Rosenberg, William Stafford, Ralph Ellison, Tom Sexton and T. L. Scott. Also, Pamela and Zara Smelcer and John Millett of South Head Press for publishing this collection.

South Head Press
The Market Place
Berrima, 2577
Australia

Contents

In Memory of my friends
who left this earth before I thanked them

William Stafford & Ralph Ellison

"All things are connected."

— Chief Seattle

CHANGING SEASONS

for James

Of course he still haunts me.

I never expected him
to jump into his grave that spring
admitting it was over.

On clear summer mornings
I still see our reflections upon the river
as my fly breaks the smooth surface.

And he walks with me in fall
when I hunt grouse in thick alder,
rifles strung heavy on bent shoulders.

For many years I will find his footprints
in fresh snow and hear him whistle
from across the frozen river.

He was always an impatient brother.

KESUGI RIDGE

for Robert Frost

Having crossed the frozen beaver
pond on yellowed snowshoes, I stop
to watch Denali pressed against a severed
moon whose quicksilver shards
slant through bent saplings

and bog spruce. Beneath this clean mantle
tussock sedge waits to turn the
tundra green, and springwater flows
like pitch through veins in swaying
birch. On this longest night, no fingers reach out

to pick ripe cloudberries. From this rise
I see a lamp in your tilted cabin
illuminate a square of fresh
fallen snow. Leaning toward wind, the only
sound the easy sweep of changing drifts
and falling snow, I imagine you bent

near that frost-lined pane; a pool of candle
wax measures lines on your page.

EASTER SUNDAY

1927. It is Easter Sunday.
A young Indian girl sits
impatient on a narrow spruce pew
inside a white-frame

church. In faded black cassock
the gaunt priest's sermon echoes
off gilded ikons of Mary and Jesus
in words distant and

unfamiliar. That evening when the child
returns home her grandmother will again
tell the story of how *Saghani Ghaay,*
Great Raven, brought light to the

world. Beyond the cabin's warmth
dusk steals across a window pane
and drifts of snow slowly form;
she stands in the night wind

turning her face up to a horn of pale moon.

THE MEAL

It is a clear evening and
Denali is close upon the blue-edged

horizon. A jay watches me from atop a ski
pushed upright into crusted snow outside the cabin

door, his careful eyes noting where crumbs fall
from the warm bread in my hand. From

above a scraggly forest of black spruce and muskeg
a raven arrives to quietly perch across the clear

cut. I do not know if his dark eyes watch me
or the soft crumbs lying on the snow-covered

porch. I return to the small wood stove
and look out the window where I see the jay

stealing his meal and the raven drifting low
over frozen marsh, disappearing in the darkening trees.

THE ROAD TO CHITINA

By the Edgerton highway, towards blue-
edged Sanford, a tattered fishwheel,
its birch basket sifting only
a tired wind.
           Near the river village,
when night fills tall shadows
like Raven's unfolding wings, a
truck rusts in an empty field.

THE PROMISE

after J. Arnett

It is carried over the distant mountain
and up the river valley
on a thick wind.
I hear it in the promise of rain
and in the forest's restless motion.

Once the moment arrives
I stand,
sloughing garments like old lives
and turn to where the river
flows dark beneath a stand of trees.

I dive into the blackness,
cold water draws me into its depths.
Rising, I pull, deliberately
towards the other side
as rain begins to fall.

On the far shore
I find nothing but myself
and the rain-soaked forest,
the gentle swinging of birch
and the bright heart of thunder.

WINTER SOLTICE ELEGY

To end this shortest day
I shoot the white-chested
caribou, down so long
she would never rise,
so tired there is no
last shiver but my own
when her bones at last drop
hard as winter boughs in wind.

In the ring of pines
steam and scent rises from the field,
freezes in air, shatters
into black birds
in a gale too steep
for the flawless sky.

At light's last breaking
I wait for a sign to release me
while watching the vanishing sun
and a small, bone-white
moon. As if expecting words
I do not have, they lie
low on either horizon, each
round as the cow's hazing eye.

LATE SEPTEMBER ON
THE RUSSIAN RIVER

The trees turn, suddenly,
as dawn rolls up what night unwound —
their slender necks
like tundra swans in shallow ponds.

There is no comforting chill
in the gray air,
only a screed of birds
scrawled on a bare sky.

Fog arrives in the narrow valley,
gray wings cupped like snow geese
landing between deserted stars
in morning's porcelain light.

A trout waves in a shadow
beneath clear water across smooth stone,
and while I watch, a bear— sleek and black—
crosses the river and fades off winterward.

GAMBELL, ST. LAWRENCE ISLAND

We're on the point
watching birds
rise above the tide out to sea.
We ask them to watch
for men.
Seven gone, eight days—
too long on a walrus hunt.
Two small boats lost in the fog
upon a desolate sea—
out of gas,
radio dead,
maybe caught in the pack ice.
For days east wind blowing hard
at Siberia.
Father Slwooko comes to sell ivory.
He says they got a walrus
for food,
water from the ice,
it's not too cold.
We ask will the search succeed.
He says, "They will have to find themselves."
We ask how long they can last
out there. He says,
"How long can a man live?"

CEREMONY

for Kenny

I bury a pine seed in a shallow field where trees are born
and turn my face up to the patient sky.

Along this river edge, so long ago, roasting salmon
on thin willows cut green from a cool shroud of forest shadow,
we could not know then as boys
how you would waste your resistance
in the quiet company of strangers and dissolution,
until it faded like your jeans and you would raise a rusted barrel
to end the fragrant memories of youth.

In the gray shade of dusk I see the black bird of your spirit
rising like a feather above the ancient river and narrow field
into a dark and rolling sundown slowly stealing
towards the blue light of a distant pink mountain.

NIGHT CROSSING

The dense forest offers a path
leading through ancient pines
circling a frozen pond
where my shadow, tall and lean,
skates along the trail behind me.

A wolf crosses from the far edge into dark wood
as night's flowing robe flails in a steep wind.

I turn from this place
with its scent of antiquity, and
setting a gait through powdery snow,
follow my shadow across a moonlit cloth.

A wolf's lonely howl rises from a distant ridge
as a hook of pale moon illuminates the thin path
ahead.

POTLATCH

for Joe Secondchief

All day they arrive at Copper Center
huddled along the frost-lined river
far from city lights
to mourn Great Uncle's death.

From the sacred circle of our clan
skin drums echo
a feeble tremor in the frozen earth.
Elder voices lament through the Great House:

'Syuu' nac'eltsiin yen
A potlatch is made for him.

Pulses quicken to the ancient rhythm.
Dancers stream like vibrations
across a wooden floor
heavy with rifles and colored blankets.

'Unggadi kanada'yaet yen ne'et dakozet
A potlatch song is sung for him in heaven.

My uncle and I fill the hollow in silence;
sombre guests depart beyond a small church.
A raven lights upon an Orthodox cross;
our thoughts are soon filled like the grave.

Tonight I have learned that there is an end
to everything, to every light—

In that end, even the yawning of brittle leaves
breaks the solititude of night.

TEX SMITH LAKE

Evening settles upon an inland lake.

I stop paddling, lightly sighing
my canoe strands in lilypads.

I hear the wind's rattling voice
from the shadowy birch behind me. The scent
of currant trails after the light collision.

A mallard comes swimming through the
green and yellow isles,
hastily, as if there is a curfew
before night cloaks the dark shore
that curves, like a yoke, into horizon.

A bubble rises and explodes softly
on the flat surface,
breaking dusk's contagious silence.

WEIR FISHER

Flowing out of green foothills
the shallow stream enters the sea.

It began its winding course
long before these banks were cut;

before Raven stole the stars and moon,
when no village stood along the shores.

Below the stone weir, an old man waits
like the hills along the creek

for what the stream will soon bring,
or what it will take away.

Once they arrive, he will lift a thin spear
while gray clouds slow the speed of light.

HWTSIIL TIDANGIYAANEN

Tadlzuun tl'ogh k'eltsiinitl'ogh dghelaay cene'
tehwdeldiyna da'snidaetl natu'.

Pedni tehwedeldiyna nilk'aedze' ghot'
tse sdaghaay ogltsii;

tse Saghani Ggaay 'cen'iis nek'e 'et nekeghaltaexi',
tse kayaxygge ogltssi tabaaghe k'eze.

Pghatsiitsen baes hwlsiil, c'etiyi ya'atse
k'e dghelaay cene' k'eze tehwdeldiyna

yenka dldaek ts'ilghu,
yen dldaek.

Pghak'ae luk'ae i'nilaex, c'etiyi nic'ayilaan glts'aek'e 'uyuunistl'en
hwna yanlae baa pk'e'e'lc'et' yikaa.

DURABLE BREATH

for Peter Kalifornsky

Outside my cabin window
I hear Raven's muffled caw rise from the river.

A lamp burns low upon my table,
the air is still in the silence of the room.

I think often of that night in your trailer at Nikiski,
of the old stories you shared with me —

Dena'ina Suk'dua
"That which is written on the people's tongues."

As a child you were beaten with a stick
for speaking your native tongue. My father,

born at Indian River,
does not know his mother's language.

Tonight, Kenaitze Indians gather
at a Russian Orthodox Church

to mourn in altered syllables among white-washed
crosses and tarnished silver ikons.

As I lean toward darkness,
it is your voice that lifts

Raven's wings above the riverbank,
his ancient syllables rising like an ochre tide.

NINILCHIK

This pebble beach and serene
moon I have seen before, when a gentle

wind failed to lift the smooth
sea, and silvery dewdrops glazed

the steep hill behind a stone-
walled harbor where Russian fishermen

from Nikolaevsk gathered near weathered
skiffs. Once, Tanaina returned here from Polly

Creek, their fish-filled boats low against a
dim horizon. Without awareness, a fine spray has

drenched me, the taste of salt fresh
upon my lips. A buoy light softly echoes in

night's coming. It is the realization
of a dream where I lingered in sadness.

RITUAL

for Charlie

The moose moves as silently as falling leaves.
Its muddy hooves blend limbs and earth
like uprooted trees — tall saplings that dust the woods
and brush the forest with their passage. Fog
fills the sky like tribal smoke rising before me.

I sit, back turned to the wind and cold,
breathing out fire that stalks within me. My
breath conjures up my father who sat in this very spot
holding the ground in place,
cradling a rifle in his arms.

I hear branches snap in my chest, twigs that break
into green bones still alive with sap. Inside
my breast, a flame flickers against winter
licking at my numbness
as my father's hand curls around my finger.

SOLSTICE

In the shadow of Denali
on summer's longest day
my young daughter

chooses smooth rocks
from a glacial stream. I take
riverwater, spoon in cocoa

to cook under birchbark. From
below the summit's crest
music from a Swainson Thrush

rises like a violin
invisible through thin air, and
holds us to every perfect

note. Almost forgotten
the red sun falls near dusk,
I turn to my cup.

We drink Denali's rugged curve, and leave
counting blue coins taken from the river's pocket.

AUTUMN

An old man bends into the weight
of a heavy axe beneath a stand of birch

gilded by sunlight. In the gathering dark
dead leaves fall upon the mirror surface

of a small lake. A boat glides
parting the leaves. From the ripples

pale stars rise like sparks above descending night.

BLACKSKIN

Dukt' ootl nudges rime from the naked tree
It sparkles on the breath of the north wind.

Morning dawns crisp and clear
There are no clouds in the pale sky.

Tidewater swells the Nass River in the early light
Rising above a red cedar mountain.

BONANZA CREEK

Years ago I came here
after the lightning burn.
Now I come alone
in search of spruce hens
hidden in the tender growth.
I go deep
into your singed forest
of birch and spruce
whose roots once drank
from the blue waters
of the rainbow trout.
And resting on a burnt log
among lupin and larkspur,
I see in the ashes
beside the fireweed
a single wild rose

TAZLINA

The summer sky is clear
save Drum's cloud-tangled summit.

No shadows darken her
silt-smoothed stones
at the confluence where she is lost
in the salmon-choked Copper
where so many fishermen soon will
line the banks at Chitina,
their long nets lifting the braided water
where once only Ahtna hung
cranberry-red salmon
on diamond willow racks
to dry in the gentle breeze
that moved like a hungry wolf
along the water's edge
to taste the river's gift.

SITKA

In Sitka, at the edge
of a dark sea, surrounded by
totem poles carved with clan histories
on red cedar, stands the
Museum of Alaska Native Art.

Years ago, a pawn shop stood here
where Tlingit men and women,
sometimes Haida too,
brought Russian trade beads to sell
for radios and whiskey,
bartered masks and art
for televisions and chain saws,
and sometimes took home
battered rifles for ceremonial dress and pipes
brought in from far villages.

After many years, when the Indians had
no more to give — nothing left to trade —
the pawnbroker wrecked his shop and built this place

which is crowded all summer with tourists eager
to see Native heritage,

and where Indians stand in line
to visit their past.

RESURRECTION

A western wind has borne my barren soul
to this sacred place
with its ancient village and rotting graves
set along the river's edge.

My lean shadow falls behind me,
disappearing in a dark forest of pine.
The river's song, rising on Eagle's slow wings,
echoes inside me.

In the past's familiar tongue
I reclaim myself.
The voice of ancestors lifts me
as I begin to heal.

The wind shifts,
its breath filling my spirit like a sail.
Resurrected, I leave at sunset
knowing I will return to this sacred earth.

HOMELAND

Anchorage, Alaska

He said his name was Harry when a white vendor told him
to stand behind the stainless cart where tourists wouldn't
see as they walked Fourth Avenue and into giftshops with
native souvenirs displayed in crowded storefronts. He
wanted change for a dollar to call his son, but was called a
drunk—"Harry, who's committing *hari kari* with booze."
That's what was said as I listened with a still warm bun in
my hand. The Indian saw me and while I traded coins he
told me how his great grand-father was a shaman whose
magic once filled Cook Inlet with shimmering salmon at a
time when fish were few. He left me alone on the noisy
street where two Germans parked a zebra-striped
motorcycle and ordered reindeer sausages, and a woman
passed with her catch of carved ivory and Eskimo masks.

THE FLEET

The gulls are hunting
in the thin fog,
the fishing fleet
moves down the inlet.
There is nothing else
but this.
In this powdery light
there is only the sea,
and the gulls
diving through the mist,
and the salmon fleet
moving into the low sun.
There is nothing
like this moment,
the water's motion
and the gull's dull gray;
nor any greater hope
than this —

these many boats
sailing out to sea.

FATHER

My Irish friend, old enough to be my father,
follows close upon the narrow footpath
to Mendeltna Creek
beyond the muskeg and frost-sheathed pond
where tundra swans will rest tonight.

So near October no grayling rise
to bend our lines taut into the icy current
flowing from Old Man Lake.

A raven shakes snow from its back
and huddles low against the slant wind
lifting a brittle leaf across the stream.

That stoic bird is you—
too hardened to complain,
as if it would somehow matter.

Fishing smooth water near your river cabin,
distant as this cold day to summer,
silence filled the void between us.

Father, that this were you beside me, the only sound
our footsteps upon the thin-layered snow.

FALLING MOON

There is a dull moon drifting on the sea,
a thin crescent
washed by ancient brine.

This fallen moon speaks to me
in the lost words
of my ancestors.

It is waning in its endless course,
staring into eternity
across an empty sea.

Tonight it mourns what has passed
and what is yet
to be lost.

This is a sacred moon,
becoming stone,
a sombre ochre.

I watch its quiet descent,
burning on the waves
before it disappears.

DADZAASI LUK'AE

for X. J. Kennedy

```
                          yen
                         ťoghe
                       yenťoghe
                  ba' zes ba' zes ba' zes
               ba' zes ba' zes  ba' zes  ba' zes ba' zes
              ba' zes ba' zes  ba' zes  ba' zes  ba' zes ba' zes
 l                ba' zes  ba' zes ba' zes ba' zes ba' zes ba' zes
 uk'        cel       ba 'zes  ba' zes  ba' zes  ba' zes  ba' zes  ba' zes  ba' zes luk' ae  zaa
 ae c     ťo g h e ba' zes ba' zes ba' zes  ba' zes  ba' zes  ba' zes  ba' zes naegge' luk' a          e
 e l a' l   ba' zes ba' zes ba' zes ba' zes ba' zes ba' zes ba' zes ba' zes ba' zes zaa luk
 uk' ae ba' zes  ba' zes  ba' zes  ba' zes  ba' zes  ba' zes  ba' zes  ba' zes 'ae z a a       lu
 cela' luk'  ba' zes  ba' zes  ba' zes  ba' zes  ba' zes  ba' zes  ba' zes  ba' zes ba' k' ae zaa luk'
 ae cel a' ba' zes ba' zes ba' zes ba' zes ba' zes ba' zes ba' zes ba' zes ba' zes  ae zaa lu
 luk' ae cel ba' zes  ba' zes  ba' zes  ba' zes ba' zes  ba' zes  ba' zes  ba' zes k'
 a' luk' ae  ba' zes ba' zes ba' zes ba' zes ba' zes ba' zes ba' zes dzaghal
 cela'lu     tsel ť     ba' zes ba' ť aay zes ba' zes ba' zes ťo g h e
 k' ae       oghe                   ťoghe                      dzagh
 c e l                              ť aay                       a l
 a'
```

40

CROW PASS

Mile 9.5

Unlacing worn leather boots, I recall
a photograph of an Indian family on the
trail through Mendeltna: Chief Stickwan's
wide face, porcupine quill necklace, broad
suspenders, and two Ahtna women
with walking sticks and battered kettles,
bent under packs like horses at

Thunderbird Falls. My ancestors,
Tatl'ahwt'aenn, these "Headwaters People"
journeyed as seasons following Nelchina
caribou in fall and netting quick-
silver salmon in summer, young
mothers sifting the Copper for its
prize to salt and dry

in smokehouses. Light softens and meltwater
flows near a small fire boiling creek
water for rosehip tea in an iron kettle
the color of Raven's eye.

CROOKED CREEK

Like perennial swallows
returning to Capistrano's white stucco
and Franciscan's in monk's
cloth the color of Raven's feathers,
two green shadows arrive
below the gentle ripples
from around a willow-tangled bend
where an eagle tears pink flesh
from a spawned and battered steelhead
against the protestations of angry gulls
screeching profanities —
having flown in from where
too many fishermen flail gray water
at the confluence where Kasilof
blends and engulfs Crooked Creek.

At Kalifornsky Village a Tanaina man
mends his worn net as tidewater rises.

SALMON ON BROADWAY

Like mountain rills after rain
they join here to gather at the light

to cross to where I stand—alone
like a turtle in the reeds.

Swirling in a slow eddy
a living current of rising tide,

driven as if by instinct
they wait like salmon to spawn

at that moment when the river
is first offered to the sea.

WILD HORSES

Makah Indian Reservation

The wild horses at Neah Bay
listen to the salted wind

bringing news of the surf
shaping Flattery's shores
beyond a verdant field and rising stream
severing me from the fibrous mustangs
and white-boned dunes on the other side.

Indian children wading tide pools in slant light
cross where red crabs scurry
from the dark of my empty shadow
to that field where black-maned horses vanish
like ghosts into tall spruce below a desert hill.

Beyond these dunes the gray Pacific
stretches its sharp-edged horizon
past waving kelp forests,
borne by sea and moon,
which will soon lie among driftwood

like ancient brine and sea shells
to be crushed by wild horses.

WINTER

for William Stafford

Shrouded in ice, the staves broke out
of the poet by twos and leap-
frogged down the frozen river in
a game of solitaire and kings.

The hands of a shadow played
white against the crystals on a slim
aspen's neck, and parlayed the
winnings into night.

I folded both palms on my stick and
watched with a croupier's eye
the invited prowl, their casino in fur;
glass at the center of clouds refracted light.

RAIN

The rain has stepped
so thoroughly into my thoughts
that I can no longer hear them.

There is no difference now between rain
and the white-capped sea.

In time, I will be unable to distinguish
even myself from the shadowy figure
the water takes on along this rocky strand.

They say the body is made of water—
born of the ancient sea.
If I but raise my weary arms tonight I could swim.

TIME

I do not know
if time is flame or flow.
I only know through the fingers it drips
leaving a hand dry and hollow,
too weak a fist to grip.

I only know how often it singes a brow,
how often youthful passions
leave a heart scorched with longing,
and burned down to a heap of ash
that a new Phoenix may arise,
its trembling wings freedom bound;

unknown if forever is fire or flood,
it neither burns up nor whirls around.

OCTOBER FROST

October and the sky is glass.

Beyond it there is little more
than that moment when the maple's burgundy leaves
touch the lowest stars and the red air burns
without remembrance of summer's wind and perfect light.

There is a blind moon overhead
as my anxious breath coats the dry grass
and first snow is squeezed
from burdened clouds.

Its falling sheds little light on the silence.

BACKROAD

I wind myself up the hill
on a slow and tattered bicycle,
one eye on the road
the other on its gravel shoulder
looking for something lost
between the beer cans
with their rusty drink of rainwater.

Somewhere there's a fire,
smoke crawls in along the valley.

Finding the top
I stop to rest my knees.

A dandelion flares up in the ditch
and rabbits vanish in thick alder.

This year they are cutting it back,
making the road harder to cross;
and in the seventh year
the asphalt is stained with indecision.

Speeding downhill, gravity pulling hard,
it is of no importance to me.

I glide for a moment
disappearing around an easy curve.

REBEL

He was the archetype
         of old rebellions,
not clearly his
or anybody's;

an entity without identity,
anger without cause
except
unrecognized
the vacuum of himself.

Between him and all glory
was a stone wall,
its rusted gates locked.

In the narrow corridor
         he turned in the dark circle of himself
and found no place to trespass,
no grass to trample.

SUMMER '69

Back then
in the trivial weather,
girls are sixteen
and boys loll at their jobs.

It is that summer forever.

And the dead are everywhere
and look forward to supper;
one is listening to a radio,
another writes a song.

But beyond September
their lives wait to begin
when they arrive.

In that perfect
pointless summer forever,
the dead everywhere
look forward to supper.

FIRST SNOW

for Zara

The window still retains tiny handprints
left by my daughter;
breath surrounding a noseprint
fades slowly.
                 Beyond porchlight,
an angel lies in new snow,
her tiny wings unfold
as if to fly above the eclipsing moon.

MEDITATION ON A SKULL

On the hill behind our cabin
I find a grizzly's skull,
fragile as a paper kite,
strangled between the matted
roots of birch and wild weeds
on autumn's forest floor.

Nothing remains
but this mottled fragment;
hungry maggots have long abandoned
the hollow of this grey and brittle bone.

In this forest without leaves
a carpenter ant crawls
through the hollow eyes
where only a slight wind
rattles in the dark hole
and the stiffening earth becomes a silent tomb.

EVENING AT FIELDING LAKE

This evening at Fielding Lake
a raven sits in thick-branched spruce
while rain clouds
move below a full moon
turning the water black.

TALT'AEZI BENE' XELTSE'E

Hwt'aedze xelts'e'de kolaexi Talt'aezi Bene'
saghani ggay ye ts' ezdaa
ts'abaeli det'en
luy'tniniltl'iits k'ay' giis kanghilyaan
tuu nelt' uuts'.

POEM FOR A RAINY DAY

A drop of water
weaves a weary path
like a web
across the glass of my window
where I watch the rain-drenched street
and slender birch
bent like old men by a tilted wind.
Above, gray clouds gather
like thoughts in my mind,
spilling into each other;
and from the light collision, sparks
burn white in the darkening sky
where only the rumble of my thoughts
like distant thunder
vanish into horizon.

TERN CREEK

I entered Tern Creek below
the slow falls to fish where the stream
began its bend before it passed
beneath the stone bridge. My
wife and I always fished
rainbows from the dark eddy
swirling beyond our feet
where I found a trout
waving in the shadows,
taking what it could off the smooth gravel.
My fly touched the surface
white line sinking into sparkling depths
I strained to see the alloy of his polished belly
in my willow creel
upon the soft pillow of green pine
boughs I cut that morning for his
bed. He reeled me
and sliced the stream,
igniting it as he ran up the falling water
with my taut line
through the powdery light
of early morning.

JACK DANIELS

Walking home, alone, half drunk
upon the rutted road,
village dogs bark, strain
at heavy chains
as the sun,
less clear than drops of night water
upon hanging leaves of Monkshood
glittering like stars and constellations,
slips along spines of conifers
into the high, cold, and distant sky
while night slides azure beyond a rising
mountain in search of another solitary edge.

THE BRASS URN

When you empty the little brass urn
that holds the dull ash that once was me
over the field of pine and wild flowers,
my wife, don't stand there in melancholy

but wipe your dim eyes,
remembering the young fingers
that wrote these lines
at a time when desire ran high

and in life touched you gently.
Take comfort in winter's porcelain light
when time falls apart in intolerable counting
and I have left the universe alone.

Photo by C. Hudson

John E. Smelcer, who was recently a Guest Native American Scholar at the Gorky Institute of World Literature in Moscow, Russia, Brooklyn College, New York and at the University of Wisconsin at Eau Claire, teaches English at Embry-Riddle Aeronautical University. He is poetry editor at Salmon Run Press where he has published many major American poets. His other books of poetry include *Kesugi Ridge, Koht'aene Kenaege'* and *The Caribou and the Stone Man.* He recently edited *Durable Breath: Contemporary Native American Poetry*, an anthology featuring forty-three established Native American poets. He appears in *Everything Matters: Autobiographical Essays By Native American Writers.* His poems have recently appeared in *The American Voice, The Atlantic Monthly, The Amicus Journal, Artful Dodge, The Beloit Poetry Journal, The Christian Science Monitor, The Kenyon Review, The Literary Review, Poet, Poets On:, Poetry Australia, Poetpourri, Permafrost, The Raven Chronicles, Rosebud, Transnational Perspectives, The Tucumcari Literary Review* and ZYZZYVA.